THE STATIONS OF THE RELIGION

First published in 2016 by

Fayda Books
3695F Cascade Rd Suite 133
Atlanta, GA 30331
www.faydabooks.com
orders@faydabooks.com

© Copyright Fayda Books 2016
ISBN 978-0-9913813-4-0

No part of this book may be reproduced in any form without prior permission of the publisher. All rights reserved.

Cover design
MUHAMMADAN PRESS
mail@muhammadanpress.com

Typesetting
ETHEREA DESIGN
enquiries@ethereadesign.com

Printed and bound in the United States

The STATIONS of the Religion

A Description of the Steps of Spiritual Wayfaring (Sulūk)

مقامات الدين الثلاث

By
Shaykh al-Islam al-Hājj
Ibrahīm b. ʿAbd-Allah Niasse

Translation by
Zachary Wright

Contents

Publisher's Preface	1
THE STATIONS OF THE RELIGION	5
Repentance	7
Steadfastness	8
God-consciousness	9
Truthfulness	10
Sincerity	11
Tranquility	12
Awareness	13
Witnessing	14
Gnosis	14
BIOGRAPHY OF SHAYKH IBRAHIM NIASSE	
Who is Shaykh Ibrahim ﷺ?	21
His Birth ﷺ	23
His Upbringing ﷺ	23
His Teaching His Students the Sciences ﷺ	24
His Entering the Tariqa ﷺ	24

His Ascendancy to the Peak and Summit of the Sciences ﷺ	26
His Excellent And Glorious Qualities ﷺ	27
The Excellence of his Poetry and Prose ﷺ	27
His Writings ﷺ	28
The Description of his Good Morals and Character ﷺ	34
His Generosity and Liberality ﷺ	37
His Move to a New Village and his Building the Zawiya of Ahl Dhikr	37
His Relation to his Father ﷺ	38
His Relation to his Mother ﷺ	39
Her Virtues, Deeds and Morals ﷺ	41

Publisher's Preface

This short book exists in order to present to the Muslim as well as non-Muslim English speaking community, a simple yet concise explanation of the "Deen" or religion called Islam. It is in fact a commentary and explanation of the famous hadith of Jibril[2], in which the blessed angel

---

2   Umar ibn al-Khattab said: One day when we were with God's messenger, a man with very white clothing and very black hair came up to us. No mark of travel was visible on him, and none of us recognized him. Sitting down before the Prophet, leaning his knees against his, and placing his hands on his thighs, he said, "Tell me, Muhammad, about submission."

He replied, 'Submission (Islām) means that you should bear witness that there is no god but God and that Muhammad is God's messenger, that you should perform the ritual prayer, pay the alms tax, fast during Ramadan, and make the pilgrimage to the House if you are able to go there."

The man said, "You have spoken the truth." We were surprised at his questioning him and then declaring that he had spoken the truth. He said "Now tell me about faith."

He replied, "Faith (Imān) means that you have faith in God, His angels, His books, His messengers, and the Last Day, and

visited the beloved Prophet ﷺ and his companions. In this visit (where he was disguised as a human-being) he asks the Prophet a series of questions, that he (Prophet Muhammad) correctly answers. At the end of the question and answer session, the Prophet reveals to his companions that the questioner was in-fact the angel Jibril, "who came to teach you your religion (Deen)."

Shaykh Ibrahim, commences in this letter/treatise to elaborate, concisely, on each of the 'stations' of the religion that are mentioned in the hadith (Islam, Iman & Ihsan)

This hadith can rightly be described as the foundation with which Muslims should undersand their goals and duties. It is in essence a complete description of the Prophet Muhammad himself.

---

that you have faith in the measuring out (of destiny), both its good and its evil."

Remarking that he had spoken the truth, he then said, "Now tell me about doing what is beautiful."

He replied, "Doing what is beautiful (Ihsān) means that you should worship God as if you see Him, for even if you do not see Him, He sees you."

Then the man said, "Tell me about the Hour"

The Prophet replied, "About that he who is questioned knows no more than the questioner."

The man said, "Then tell me about its marks."

He said, "The slave girl will give birth to her mistress, and you will see the barefoot, the naked, the destitute, and the shepherds vying with each other in building."

Then the man went away. After I had waited for a long time, the Prophet said to me, "Do you know who the questioner was, 'Umar?" I replied, "God and His messenger know best. "He said, "He was Gabriel. He came to teach you your religion. "
(Muslim)
40 Hadith Nawawi (hadith 2)

We hope this book can serve as an instructional reminder for those that seek perfection.

May Allah bless our guides, may he benefit us by them and may we draw closer to Himself and his beloved Messenger. Amin

Ibrahim Ahmed Dimson
PUBLISHER, FAYDA BOOKS

The Stations of the Religion

Shaykh Ibrāhīm drafted the following letter concerning the "three stations of the religion" (maqāmāt al-dīn al-thalāth) on his farm outside of Kaolack in 1931.[2] It has since served as a significant public description of the steps of spiritual wayfaring (sulūk).

In the Name of Allāh, the Compassionate, the Merciful, and may Allāh's blessing be upon His noble Prophet Muḥammad, the best of humanity, and upon his companions, the stars (of guidance).

All praise is due to Allāh, the Peace, the Security, the Beneficent, glory be to Him. He is the King, the Forgiving, the Merciful, the Watchful, the Protector.

Peace be upon (Muḥammad) the straight path, the God-conscious one, the pure, the truthful, the sincere, the one molded with tremendous character, the observant, the witness, the source of most perfect gnosis, the servant (ʿabd) and the master (sayyid), the one described with the attributes of the Greatest Master. May Allāh's complete satisfaction be upon the helper of the Truth by the Truth, the guide to the straight path, and on his

---

2 Niasse, *Jawāhir al-rasāʾil*, III: 50-55.

people, (may this prayer be) worthy of his merit, and surely his worth is exceedingly great.

I have received your noble letter and greetings of peace, most agreeable beloved and exemplary seeker of (Divine) satisfaction, ʿUmar b. Mālik, may the Sovereign treat both you and your father with kindness. I received your question concerning the three stations of the Religion (*maqāmāt al-dīn*), the abodes that pertain to them, and the reality of these properties. This matter has been discussed with extensive research by the master, the knower of Allāh, ʿUbayda b. Anjūba, in his book *Mīzāb (al-raḥma)*.[3] But since you did not find what suffices you therein, here is what has been possible for me to write down of my thoughts:

There is nothing worthy of worship but Allāh (*lā ilāha ill-Allāh*). The stations of the Religion are three: submission (*islām*), faith (*īmān*), and excellence (*iḥsān*). *Islām* is the pronouncement of "There is nothing worthy of worship but Allāh." *Īmān* is to have knowledge of "There is nothing worthy of worship but Allāh." *Iḥsān* is the course in accordance with "There is nothing worthy of worship but Allāh." This means that you pronounce the words of a spiritual state, the speech of Allāh, the noble word; which is the word of repentance, the word of God-consciousness, the word of sincerity, the word of Divine Unity, the good word. This (statement) has three degrees. The first degree is the station of *Islām*, which is undertaking the emulation of the wise statement on this lowest plane of material existence (*ḥaḍra al-nāsūt*). The second degree, *Īmān*, is the knowledge of

---

3 Further discussion of Ibn Anjūba's discussion of the *Maqāmāt al-dīn* can be found in Rüdiger Seesemann, *The Divine Flood: Ibrāhīm Niasse and the Roots of a Twentieth-Century Sufi Revival* (Oxford UP, 2010), 87-91.

this statement, and the third degree, *Iḥsān*, is (being) the speech of Allāh. Thus the three stations can be explained as all revolving around the statement, "There is nothing worthy of worship but Allāh."

REPENTANCE

As for the "abodes" (*manāzil*), the first abode of Islām is repentance (*tawba*). This means removing oneself from denying blessing. Having gratitude and consideration for every blessing is a means of attaining the satisfaction of the Benefactor, and the opposite of gratitude is disbelief (*kufr*). The Sufi scholars have added that repentance is leaving aside base character traits for sublime character traits. I would add that base character traits for the common people include leaving aside the obligations of the Religion (*farāʾiḍ*) and pursuing forbidden things. The baseness of the elite is to leave aside the supererogatory exemplary acts (*faḍāʾil*) while pursuing reprehensible things (*makrūhāt*). The baseness of the elite of the elite is the turning away from the Divine Presence (*ḥaḍra*), which constitutes heedlessness.

This form of repentance is the reality of repentance, because real repentance means to kill the lower self (*nafs*), as the Most High said, "*So repent to your Creator, and kill your (lower) selves.*"[4] (True repentance is when) one does not perceive the repentance, nor perceive anything belonging to it; neither action, nor spiritual station, nor station. This is repentance from repentance: "*Surely Allāh loves the repentant.*"[5] In other words, (those who repent) from repentance.

---

4 Qurʾān, 2:54.
5 Qurʾān, 2:222.

STEADFASTNESS

The second (abode of Islām) is steadfastness (*istiqāma*), which means traveling (*sulūk*) the straight path without deviation from the structure of the path. Allāh, Blessed and Exalted is He, enumerated ten qualities of the straight path in the "Chapter of the Cattle (*Sūrat al-Anʿām*) by His statement:

> *Say, "Come, I will recite that which your Lord has made a sacred duty on you: that you do not associate anything as a partner with Him, that you be good to your parents; that you do not kill your children because of poverty – it is We who provide for you and them; that you do not approach shameful deeds, whether openly or secretly; and that you do not take human life which Allāh has made sacred, except in the course of legal justice. This He has commanded you, so that you may discern.*
>
> *Do not come near to the orphan's property, except to improve it, until he reaches maturity. Give full measure and weight, in justice. We do not burden any soul beyond its capacity. And if you give your word, do justice to it, even though it be (against) a kinsman; and fulfill the covenant of Allāh. This He has commanded you, so that you may remember.*
>
> *Verily this is My straight path, so follow it. Do not follow other ways, they will sever you from His way.*[6]

So the goal of the straight path as designated is action, putting in practice these properties. The first is not associating partners with Allāh; then not taking the life

---

6   Qurʾān, 6:151-153.

Allāh has made sacred, not killing one's children fearing poverty, abandoning shameful deeds whether openly or secretly, and so forth. The steadfastness of the common folk is thus fulfilling the rights of the straight path.

For the elite, steadfastness is traveling the straight path, while the Messenger of Allāh, peace and blessings upon him, is with them. So this means annihilation in the Prophet, along with (annihilation in) loving him and his character, thus molding oneself with his character, both openly and secretly. This entails busying oneself with his remembrance, invoking blessings on him, and praying for him in every breath. This is the steadfastness mentioned in the statement of the Most High, *"Those who say our Lord is Allāh, and are steadfast, the Angels descend on them, saying, 'Do not fear nor grieve, but listen to the good tidings of the Paradise promised you.'"*[7]

The steadfastness of the elite of the elite is that nothing of the creation persists in you, even if concealed; and what is repulsive (*khabīth*) is completely unknown. This steadfastness is more comprehensive than the general steadfastness, since normally affairs fall into various categories: obligatory, preferred, neutral, disliked, and forbidden.

GOD-CONSCIOUSNESS

The third (abode of Islām) is the fear of Allāh (*taqwā*), which means carrying out the commandments and avoiding the prohibitions, openly and secretly, publicly and privately. So complete implementation of the commandments and complete avoidance of the prohibitions is the fear of the common folk. Among the elite, fear of Allāh is to remember Him and not to forget Him, to obey

---

7   Qurʾān, 41:30.

Him and not to disobey Him. The Most High said, "*O you who believe, fear Allāh as He should be feared.*"⁸ This refers to the degree of the elite (in God-consciousness), just as the Most High's statement, *"Fear Allāh as much as you can,"*⁹ refers to the degree of the common folk.

The fear of the elite of the elite is when nothing occurs to the mind except by Allāh even for a single moment. The gnostic says, "If other than You should occur to my mind, it is a selfish desire afflicting my thought, heedlessly, for which I would be guilty of apostasy (*ridda*)." But this is the spiritual state (*ḥāl*) of the gnostic and the spiritual station (*maqām*) of the unique and comprehensive saintly pole (*al-quṭb al-fard al-jāmiʿ*). The poet is here speaking of his spiritual state, but this (permanent) state of mind is not incumbent on the (ordinary) gnostic. This type of fear is alluded to in Allāh's saying, "*Surely Allāh loves the God-fearing.*"¹⁰

TRUTHFULNESS

The second station of the Religion is the station of Īmān (faith). Its first abode is truthfulness (*ṣidq*), which is working righteousness seeking the Countenance of Allāh the Most High. He said:

> *Righteousness is having faith in Allāh, the Last Day, the Angels, the Scripture, and the Prophets; and to give of your wealth, for love of Him, to your kin, to the needy, to the traveler, to those who ask, and for freeing slaves; and to establish the prayer and to pay the poor-due; and to fulfill the contracts you have made; and to*

---

8 Qurʾān, 3:102.
9 Qurʾān, 64:16.
10 Qurʾān, 3:76.

> *be patient in tribulation, adversity, and time of stress. Such are the truthful ones.*[11]

Such is the truthfulness of the common folk.

The truthfulness of the elite is the truthfulness in the love of Allāh's Exalted Essential Being (*al-dhāt al-ʿaliyya*). Arrival to the Exalted Essential Being becomes more beloved to him than everything in existence, and Allāh's Name is more beloved to him than any name, and Allāh's Speech is more beloved than any other words, and Allāh's satisfaction is more beloved to him than any other satisfaction, and Allāh's beloveds (*aḥbāb*) are more beloved to him than his own beloveds. So this is the truthfulness of the elite, and the Most High said, "*Be among the truthful ones.*"[12] The person who has attained this station does not attach his mind to the love of anything unless Allāh desires that he find it. The mind of the truthful person does not become attached to anything that Allāh does not want to exist for him. "*And that is the bounty of Allāh, which He gives to whom He wills, and Allāh is the possessor of great bounty.*"[13]

The truthfulness of the elite of the elite is to attest (*taṣdīq*) to everything conveyed to the Prophetic Presence from the Divine Presence; whether knowledge, spiritual state, secrets, conduct, rights, or duties. Whoever attains truthfulness to this degree possesses the best form of truthfulness.

SINCERITY

The second (abode of faith) is sincerity (*ikhlāṣ*). Sincerity is to act upon the commandments and to forsake the

---

11 Qurʾān, 2:177.
12 Qurʾān, 9:119.
13 Qurʾān, 57:21.

prohibitions for the sake of Allāh's Noble Countenance, for if you find in yourself any ostentation, concern for reputation, or vanity, you have not attained sincerity. This is the sincerity of the common folk.

The sincerity of the elite is to put the Religion into practice, not for the sake of reward, nor for fear of punishment, nor for attaining to a spiritual station (*maqām*). Rather, you worship Allāh out of yearning (for Him). Worship (*ʿubūdiyya*) means that you put the Religion into practice for no other reason than the fact Allāh deserves to be worshipped, and you are a servant for whom nothing else is fitting besides service. So you act for His sake, and you do not perceive yourself deserving anything from Him. You give witness to the blessing, and He gives witness to your good deeds. Indeed, such deeds are from Him to you. He created them, and attributed them to you from His grace and blessing.

The sincerity of the elite of the elite is to banish all otherness in your dealing with the Real (*al-Ḥaqq*), and surely your own self (*nafs*) is among the otherness so banished. Like this you will perceive that all works (*ʿamal*) are from Allāh, to Allāh, and by Allāh. You have no entry in them and no exit from them. Know that Allāh loves (such) sincere ones.

TRANQUILITY

The third (abode of faith) is tranquility (*ṭumaʾnīna*). Tranquility is the stillness of the heart with Allāh, its sufficiency in Allāh from everything else, and its dwelling (*baqāʾ*) with Allāh. Youthful speculations as to what will benefit or harm the self no longer exist in the heart. Rather the soul (*nafs*) has become calm in Allāh's Hands. The tongue of this spiritual state says, "O Allāh, on You is my reliance..."[14] This is the meaning of tranquility, but it is not possible except for the elite. The tranquility of the elite of the elite consists in their certain knowledge that there is nothing other than Allāh in existence. The soul of such a person does not rest except in Him, and does not return except to Him, and its address from Allāh is "*O soul in tranquility, return to Your Lord.*"[15]

AWARENESS

The third station of the Religion is spiritual excellence (*iḥsān*). Its first abode is awareness (*murāqaba*), which is continuous presence with Allāh. The knowledge gained by His acquaintance permeates the entirety of the servant, so that this notion (of Divine proximity) never leaves him. The reality is disclosed to him from behind a subtle veil, so he gains experiential understanding. The one who arrives to this station may speak words that do not reflect the perfect specification of the spiritually arrived, for he has not fully arrived since the reality is disclosed to him from behind a subtle veil. He takes knowledge by means of understanding and experience, not direct witnessing. So this is the awareness of the elite before witnessing. The awareness after witnessing is the awareness of the elite of the elite. This awareness is most precious, and is a station among the stations of the spiritually distinguished (*al-rijāl*), the result of gnosis.

---

14   This is a reference to an important supplication of the Tijāniyya order (see Muḥammad al-Ḥāfiẓ al-Tijānī, *Aḥzāb wa awrād* (Dakar: al-Maktaba al-Islāmiyya, unknown date), 139-140) used by Shaykh Ibrāhīm Niasse for the spiritual training (*tarbiya*) of disciples. See the section on supplications later in this book.
15   Qurʾān, 89:27-28.

WITNESSING

The second (abode of *ihsān*) is witnessing (*mushāhada*), which is the ocular vision of the Real by the Real, without misgiving, doubt, or delusion. This is because nothing remains except the Real, by the Real, in the Real. So long as a single hair of the servant should remain in existence, he will not arrive to this station. Nay, he must pass away from himself, from all otherness and concern for what is other. The tongue of this spiritual state says, "Nothing remains except Allāh, nothing other than Him; so there is no object of arrival, and nothing to be made clear." Here there is no name and no description, no designation and no delimitation. This vision is without explanation, and it has no differentiation and no union, no direction and no reception, no beginning, no connection, and no separation. There is no remembrance, no one performing the remembrance, and no object of remembrance. "*Truth has come and falsehood has perished. Surely falsehood is ever bound to perish.*"[16]

This degree is the closest of degrees to the spiritual opening (*fath*), and what came before this was not by such opening. Witnessing is the door of gnosis (*ma'rifa*), but it is not gnosis. Every gnostic has been opened, but not every opened one is a gnostic.

GNOSIS

The third (abode of *ihsān*) is gnosis (*ma'rifa*), which is when the spirit becomes thoroughly familiar with and fixed in the presence of (Divine) witnessing, with complete annihilation (*fanā'*) and subsequent remaining (*baqā'*) by Allāh. The gnostic according to the Sufis is the one who either sees otherness as the Essence (*'ayn*), or

---

16 Qur'ān, 17:81.

who witnesses the Real in otherness. But the gnostic with me is the one who finds annihilation once in the Divine Essence (*dhāt*), and in the Attribute two or three times. So he finds annihilation in the Name once, and bears witness to the existence through the three (Attributed) Realities, bearing witness to the Names by the Name. This is a station that would require stripping the thornbush of its leaves and the shredding of internal organs, but it is not obtained by sacrifice of wealth and children.[17] The resident of this station is completely awake to Allāh, His wisdom and His rulings. He is content with the manifestation of the decrees of Divine ordainment. He has obtained a perfect contentment with Allāh, so Allāh is contented with him. His soul (*nafs*) is thus worthy of being addressed by the words of the Most High: "*So enter the company of My (honored) servants, and enter My Paradise.*"[18]

Gnosis is the last station of the Religion while repentance (*tawba*) is the first. Even still, repentance is better than gnosis since (true) repentance is the result of gnosis. This is because the reality of repentance is to be absent from repentance. For this reason Shaykh Tijānī, the Seal of Saints, may Allāh be pleased with him, used to say, "I swear by Allāh – other than whom there is no god – I did not reach the station of repentance (*maqām al-tawba*)." He meant, may Allāh be pleased with him, that he had repented from seeing his own repentance, for so long as the servant sees the repentance belonging to himself, he has not reached the station of repentance…

---

17 In other words, it is a station only obtained through Allāh's favor. I thank Moctar Ba for relating to me the interpretation of this sentence from Shaykh Baye Ould al-Haiba, interview, Medina-Baye Senegal, 3 January, 2015.
18 Qurʾān, 89:30.

The reality of repentance is the repentance from repentance, for "surely Allāh is He who accepts repentance, theMerciful."[19]

The reality of steadfastness (*istiqāma*) is the remaining (*baqā'*) after annihilation (*fanā'*): "*Verily, Allāh ordains what He wills.*"[20]

The reality of fear (*taqwā*) is the absence of thought unless it comes from the Divine Mind (*al-khāṭir*), even for a single moment: "*That is because Allāh is the Real.*"[21]

The reality of truthfulness (*ṣidq*) is the singular devotion to Allāh: "*Everything will perish except His Countenance.*"[22]

The reality of sincerity (*ikhlāṣ*) is that you do not see good deeds proceeding from you, returning to you, or being owned by you. Whatever is in the heavens and earth is from Him. "*To Him return all affairs.*"[23] "*His is the sovereignty, to Him belongs all praise.*"[24]

The reality of tranquility (*tuma'nīna*) is that you do not wish for the end of what is, nor the existence of what is not. "*Surely Allāh knows and you do not know.*"[25] "*He is not asked about what He does.*"[26]

The reality of awareness (*murāqaba*) is the ceaseless attachment of the heart to Allāh. "*Verily, your Lord is ever watchful.*"[27] "*And there is no affair in which you are engaged, no portion of the Qur'ān which you recite, and no deed that you are doing, except that We are witness*

---

19 Qur'ān, 9:104.
20 Qur'ān, 5:1.
21 Qur'ān, 31:30.
22 Qur'ān, 28:88.
23 Qur'ān, 42:53.
24 Qur'ān, 64:1.
25 Qur'ān, 16:74.
26 Qur'ān, 21:23.
27 Qur'ān, 89:14.

over you while you are engaged in it."[28] "*And We know what his soul whispers to him, for We are closer to him than his jugular vein.*"[29] "*There is no secret council of three except that He is the fourth of them.*"[30] "*Surely Allāh is the one knowledgeable of what is in the hearts.*"[31]

The reality of witnessing (*mushāhada*) is the vision of the Real with the eyes: "*Everywhere you turn, there is the Countenance of Allāh.*"[32]

The reality of gnosis (*maʿrifa*) is the direct witnessing of the perfection of the Divine Being (*al-kamāl al-dhātī*). "*There is nothing like to Him.*"[33]

---

28 Qurʾān, 10:61.
29 Qurʾān, 50:16.
30 Qurʾān, 58:7.
31 Qurʾān, 3:154.
32 Qurʾān, 2:115.
33 Qurʾān, 42:11.

Biography of Shaykh Ibrahim Niasse

Written by
Shaykh Saydi Ali Cisse

بِسْمِ اللَّهِ الرَّحْمَٰنِ الرَّحِيمِ

In the Name of Allah the Compassionate the Merciful

O Allah! Send peace and blessings upon the Secret of the Essence *(sirr al-dhat)* and the Interpreter of the Names and the Attributes *(tarjuman al-asma wa's sifat)*, our Master Muhammad, the best of creation and upon his Family and his Companions, the fountains of virtue and bounty. What follows: this is only a (brief) summary and outline of the author's biography:

WHO IS SHAYKH IBRAHIM ?

He is the Shaykh in all his degrees; the tongue of his time and the light of his age *(lisan waqtihi wa nur zamanihi)*; unique in his kind *(nasij wahdihi)*; the focal point of Allah's sight among His creation *(mahal nadhr Allah min khalqhi)*; the open door for all who desire to enter the Presence of His Holiness; unique and peerless in his era in knowledge and *Deen (farid dahrihi fi'l ilm wa deen)*; the Shaykh of his epoch in the spiritual training of the disciples *(tarbiyya't al-muridin)*; the flag and standard of the rightly-guided and the seal of those who have experienced the reality of things *('Alama al-muhtadin wa khatim al-muhaqqiqin)* in the 14th century *(hijri)*; the joy and delight of the days and the nights *(bahja't layali wa'l ayam)*; the proof of the renowned Gnostics of Allah *(hujjat'l 'arifin al-a'lam)*; the pinnacle of the

Muhammadan Ummah; the helper of the Tariqa Ahmadiyya-Ibrahimiyya-Hanifiyya and the cream of its most exalted men; the sunrise of knowledge and gnosis *(matali'a shamsh'l 'ulum wa'l ma'arif)*; the conjoiner of intellects and intuitions; the impenetrable fortress and exalted cave; the pearl of the crown of the noble *Siddiqin*; the medium by which the priceless necklace of the eminent *Qutbs* is conveyed *(wasita al-'aqd an-nafis min al-Aqtab al-a'lam)*; the bearer of the flags of nobility and dignity among humanity; the restorer of the knowledge of the People *(the Sufis)*—which had been completely separated and broken off—from the beginning of this *Ummah* until now.

He is gifted with a well-pleasing beautiful character and the sacred Muhammadan attributes *(akh al-akhlaq al-hasanat'l mardiyya wa shama'il al-qudsiyya Muhammadiyya)*; Endowed with the highest degree of Divine knowledge and Lordly Beneficence and Gnosis-whereby no eloquent and copious speech can describe, as a bounty and favor from the Generous, the Bestower *(fadlan wa tafdilan min al-Karim al-Wahhab)*; He is without equivalent or comparison in the present as well as the future *('adim an-nadhir wa'l mithal fi'l hal wa'l ma'al)*; He ascended the summit and peak of honor, distinction, purity and perfection by means of the Muhammadan inheritance and the *Ahmadi-Khatimi* spiritual training *(tarbiyya)*; He is the one adorned with the crowns of beautiful jewels; the Owner of hidden signals, tremendous utility and benefit and enlightening communications *(sahib al-isharat al-khafiyya wa'l ifadat al-adhima wa'l 'ibarat al-mafhama)*.

He is our Shaykh and our means of approach to Allah; the unique Lordly Cardinal Pole *(al-Qutb al-fard ar-rabbani)*; the great Eternal Gnostic *(al-'arif al-kabir as-samdani)*—Shaykh Ibrahim ibn Al-Hajj Abdullahi al-Tijani ibn Sayyid Muhammad ibn Mudamba ibn Bakr ibn Muhammad al-Amin ibn Samba ibn ar-Rida—may Allah be pleased with them all and may He benefit us and our loved ones by him! Ameen!

HIS BIRTH

He was born on Thursday (after *Salatul 'Asr*) in the middle of the month of *Rajab* in the year *1320h* /1902 in *"Tayba-Niassene"*, a village which was built by his father (may Allah be pleased with him). It should suffice you as proof of its excellence and virtue, as well as the authenticity of its name, which means "Purity & Goodness", due to its being the birthplace of this Honorable Imam—the owner of grand eminence.

HIS UPBRINGING

He grew up under the supervision and care of his father (may Allah be pleased with him)-the possessor of virtue, modesty, righteousness, piety, manliness, propriety, good morals and godliness. He studied The Qur'an, according to the reading *(riwaya)* of Imam Warsh on the authority of Nafi', under his father, until he memorized it completely with a perfect memorization. The signs of nobility had become apparent in him while he was still a youth owing to his readiness and willingness to help and assist. He exerted his effort and sincere undertaking to acquire the official and formal sciences *(al-'ulum ar-rasmiyya)*, their literal texts and its proper understanding, until he reached and achieved the intended goal. He studied them exhaustively and mastered all their disciplines, being the head of the class in a short time. Allah had established him as a mercy for His servants and as a benefit for every town dweller and Bedouin nomad.

His schooling was provided by his father, the owner of firmly established credentials and a well-known reputation, until he received from him, praise is due to Allah, the precious gems of useful lessons and the gifts of the secrets, the invocations and the customary practices *(fara'id al-fawa'id wa silat al-asrar wa'l adhkar wa'l 'awā'id)*. Then Allah granted him a complete Opening and Victory *(thumma fathaha Allah alayhi fathan tamma)* and bestowed upon him knowledge from His Divine Presence until he became consummate in them. He did not study them under anyone, for he was taught by none but The One Who knows all things *(al-'alim)* by Divine inspiration.

HIS TEACHING HIS STUDENTS THE SCIENCES

He did not cease being diligent and assiduous in acquiring and dispensing beneficial knowledge until many people began coming to him hopeful and in search of such. They received benefit from his school *(madrasa)*, along with the erudite scholars who also received training at his hand, as is witnessed on his behalf by the people of gnosis and knowledge *(ahl al-diraya wa'l 'irfan)*. His blessing thus increased to all the brethren and his rank and degree was exalted above all contemporaries.

HIS ENTERING THE TARIQA

He received the Tariqa Tijaniyya from the unique of his age; the proof of the people of his era; the *Zamzam* of its litanies *(Awrad)* and secrets *(asrar)*; the unifier of its lights *(anwar)* and remembrances *(adhkar)*, his Shaykh and his father, the erudite scholar and helpful model and exemplar, the *Khalifa* of Shaykh Tijani without doubt and the bearer of the flag of his Tariqa in the lands of the

West *(bilad al-gharb)*. He is the Shaykh, the Imam, and one of the eminent Saints; the one who joins the Sacred Law *(Shari'a)* with Absolute Reality *(Haqiqa),* becoming thereby a guide of the Tariqa, Al-Hajj Abdullahi ibn Sayyid Muhammad (may his Generous Lord not cease to promote him to the *Ahmadi* station). Then after entering the Tariqa, his perfect, upright, serene, well-pleasing and well-pleased soul was filled with ardent yearning *(himma)* and he experienced an increase in his lofty aspiration to the point that had he directed it towards firmly established mountains they would have crumbled instantly! His desire and longing was for harvesting the fruits of Divine and Real Knowledge and tasting the Heavenly Kingdom and the Spiritual Secrets *(al-'ulum al-haqāniya wa'l adhwāq al-Malakutiyya wa'l asrar al-Jabarutiyya)*, to such an extent that no one before or after him could even hope to reach!

By Allah! How wonderful are these verses of the moving speaker and erudite scholar, the poet, al-Khandidh, in which he praises this Shaykh (may Allah be pleased with him) in his *"al-Nuniyya"*:

> *He is the well-known Qutb of the Tariqa Tijaniyya and its crown,*
> *Its Imam and his good fortunes are its crown.*
> *The owner of the highest degree, beneath which the Gnostics are ranked—*
> *even if their gnosis ('irfan) is elevated.*
>
> *By him the status of the Sacred Law (Shari'a) has been enhanced,*
> *and through him the eminence of Absolute Reality (Haqiqa) has been made prominent.*
> *The evidence and trace of both, but for him, would be extremely faint and unclear among*

> *humanity, and their pillars and supports would be demolished."*

Then he proceeded with the duty of benefiting creation with the knowledge which is bestowed from the Divine Presence and the Lordly intuitive Gnosis *(al-ma'arif ar-rabbaniyya)*, devoting himself to the mission in his nights and his days, his mornings and his evenings.

HIS ASCENDANCY TO THE PEAK AND SUMMIT OF THE SCIENCES

As for the Book and the Sunna, good morals, education, right-guidance, oratorical proficiency, fluency, and eloquence, he feasted on them to such an extent that anyone else was the uninvited guest at his table where they were concerned. This has been witnessed on his behalf by the people of culture and refinement of his time, those nearby and those far away. Whenever he spoke, the articulate and fluent Arabs *(fusaha' al-'arab)* would fall on their knees in front of him, raising their heads and lending him their ears. In his hand was the rein and bridle of the entirety of the traditional and intellectual sciences *(al-'ulum al-'aqliyya wa'l naqliyya)*, so he would decipher their meanings as he willed and extract the pearls from their treasure-troves on the spur of the moment.

As for the Lordly Realities, the Sacred intuitive Gnosis and the Essential spiritual states ,*(al-haqa'iq ar-rabbaniyya wa'l ma'arif al-qudsiyya wa'l ahwal ad-dhatiyya)* he was the carrier of their flag, the key to their doors, their niche, their lamp and their crystal *(mishkatuha wa misbahuha wa zujajuha)*. To him belongs numerous excellent virtues and merits!

HIS EXCELLENT AND GLORIOUS QUALITIES

As for his excellent and superior qualities and the abundance of his benefit for the creation of his Lord, we are frozen, so neither the pen nor the tongue can sufficiently describe them! Indeed, he suckled the breast of excellence, good morals and independent judgment *(ijtihad)*, seeking the pleasure of The Generous and Beneficent Master *(al-mawla al-hanan wa'l manan)*, for the benefit and consolation of the poor and needy indigents, as well as the affluent. So he grew up on the love of that breast-feeding until his reputation soared and his mention became widespread on the horizons. The banners of primacy *(rāyāt as-sabaq)* were anchored in his presence without dispute, controversy or dissension. He never ceased to be the giver of gracious favors and bounties and the patron of generous blessings in every moment and time, therefore the fragrance and scent of his bounties, generosity and beneficence were spread everywhere. In short, his excellent and glorious qualities cannot be enumerated, for the records could never completely count his virtue, even if all the pens were used until they broke on the sheets of paper!

THE EXCELLENCE OF HIS POETRY AND PROSE

As for the excellence of his poetry and his prose, his mastery of the skills of rhetoric and expression, and the eloquent use of the pen and the tongue—Sahban and Hassan could not have matched him!

HIS WRITINGS

He is the author of numerous books, reports, beneficial replies and useful letters, in which he resolves the differences in the texts of the Imams, who are reliable sources of guidance. Among his writings are the following:

1. *Kashf al-Ilbas 'an Fayda 't al-Khatm Abu'l Abbas*
   The Removal of the Cloak from the Bountiful Grace of the Seal Abu'l Abbas

2. *Musarat'l Majāmi' fi Masa'il al-Jāmi'*
   The Charm of the Compositions concerning the Issues of the Compositor

3. *Al-Khamr al-Halal fi Madh Sayyid ar-Rijal*
   The Lawful Wine concerning the Praise of the Master of Men

4. *Taisir al-Wusul ila Hadrat ar-Rasul*
   The Easy Facilitation of Attainment to the Presence of the Messenger

5. *Tayyib al-Anfas fi Mada'ih al-Khatm Abu'l Abbas*
   The Fragrance of the Breaths concerning the Praise of the Seal Abu'l Abbas

6. *Rawd al-Muhhabin fi Madh Sayyid al-'Arifin*
   The Garden of the Lovers concerning the Praise of the Master of the Gnostics

7. *Nur ar-Rabbani fi Madh Sayyid Ahmad al-Tijani*
   The Lordly Light concerning the Praise of Sidi Ahmad al-Tijani

8. *Ruh al-Adab lima hawā min Hukm wa Adab*
   The Spirit of Good Morals because of what it Contains of Wisdom and Good Morals

9. *Nur al-Basr fi Madh Sayyid al-Bashr*
   The Light of the Eye concerning the Praise of the Master of Mankind

10. *As-Sirr al-Akbar wa Kibrit al-Ahmar*
    The Greatest Secret and the Red Sulfur

11. *Tuhfat al-Atfal fi Haqa'iq al-Af'al*
    The Treasure of the Children concerning the Real Meaning of Verbs in Conjugation

12. *Al-Fayda 't Ahmadi fi'l Mawlid al-Muhammadi*
    The Ahmadi Flood concerning the Birth of Muhammad

13. *Tabsira't al-Anam fi an al-'Ilm huwa al-Imam*
    The Enlightenment of Mankind concerning the fact that Knowledge is the Leader

14. *Ruh al-Hubb fi Madh al-Qutb*
    The Spirit of Love concerning the Praise of the Cardinal Pole

As for the evidence of his virtuous merit, excellence and superiority; the exaltedness of his degree and value; the height of his aspiration and yearning *(rafa'at himmatuhu)*, it should suffice you as proof that Allah made him to be a well and fountain for the spiritual-minded *(manhalan lil wāridin),* caused him to be a means of hope for the disciples and the seekers *(mu'ilan lil muridin as-sālikin),* established him as a support for those seeking aid and help, and made him an assistant for the destitute and nourishment for the starving *(thafran lil 'āfina wa qutan lil murmilin)*. Allah also favored him with the *Fayda,* or Spiritual Effusion, which was spoken of by the Hidden Cardinal Pole and the well-known Muhammadan Seal *(Qutb al-Maktum wa'l Khatm al-Muhammadi al-Ma'lum)*-our Shaykh and our support, the father of Bountiful Grace, our master Ahmad ibn Muhammad al-Tijani, for it has spread and continued without interruption due to its appearance at the end of the age *(akhir az-zaman)*. At his hand, thousands upon thousands have attained the perfection of *Ma'rifa,* or Divine Gnosis and direct intuitive knowledge *(kamāl al-ma'rifat 'iyāaniya't shuhudiya)*. Everyday many people would come to him, both whites and blacks, entering our Tariqa Tijaniyya, the essence of Lordly endowments and mystical gifts *(dhat al-manaha ar-rabbaniya wa'l mawahib al-'irfaniya),* coming from every region of the earth in droves and droves. No single person took this intensely profound litany *(wird al-jasim)* from him without gaining the benefit of Lordly help and support *(madad ar-rabbaniya),* as well as access to the realms of Gnosis and direct intuitive knowledge *(hulul mawatan al-'irfan)*. Allah has caused the author of the poem quoted above (Al-Khandidh) to gush and flow copiously when he said:

> *You have smoothed the hard ground of the Path (tariq) for your disciple,*
> *so its rocks are not feared, nor its boulders.*
> *You are the Imam, its leader and its physician (tabibuha),*
> *Its guide, its Luqman, its Sultan.*
> *To you belong its subjects and its Caesar,*
> *Its Anushirwan, its Negus and its Khanqan.*

He (may Allah be pleased with him) was the firm and upright carrier of the load and burden of the Prophetic-Muhammadan spiritual training *(tarbiyya an-nabawiyya't Muhammadiyya)* in his time; the holder of the *Ahmadi-Ibrahimi* flag of promotion and advancement; the temple of the secrets, spiritual experiences, lights, spiritual states and stations and the concluding manifestations *(haykal al-asrar wa'l adhwaq wa'l anwar wa'l ahwal wa'l maqamāt wa'l tajaliyāt'l khitmiyya)*. You have evidence of this in the fact that some of the chief sons of our leaders and guides and *'Alawi* Shaykhs came to him to join and enter his company, obtain his guidance, cling to his coat-tail and to receive the Tijani *wird*. Such as: The offspring of our Shaykh and our means of approach to Allah, Shaykh Muhammad al-Hafiz, who spread the Tariqa in the lands of the Far West *(Maghrib al-Aqsa)* and the children of his *Khalifa* and son-in-law, Sidi Muhamdi; The children of Shaykh Mawlud Fal; The children of Shaykh Muhammad Fal; and the children of Shaykh Muhammad al-Hanafi.

He cultivated and refined them with an excellent spiritual training *(rabbahum ahsana tarbiyya),* guided them along the Straight Path and Tariqa, and presented them before their Lord and Master in a perfect state, entering the protection of His Fold, intoxicated by the wine of His Presence, annihilated to their own existence and surviving in perpetuity in Him *(fānina 'an wujudihim bāqina bihi)*. Congratulations and more belong to these exceptional Masters for their holding to the coat-tail of this guiding Shaykh and trainer *(shaykh al-murshid al-murabbi)*, and for not allowing their ancestral relations to the Shaykhs to obstruct them from reaching the Perfected One of the age *(kāmil al-'asr)*. It is ancestral relationship to the Shaykhs that has hindered and impeded many of our contemporaries, as it did others among the people of ancient times. O Allah! remove the veil from us and relieve us of the attachments and blockages just as You have done for those who possess understanding—the people of sincerity and certitude *(dhu'l al-bab ahl tasdiq wa'l yaqin)*. Raise us to the highest station at all times! Grant every success and victory to those who perceive and recognize this Shaykh, keep his company and believe in him, as well as those who see him, submit to him and do not disobey him! Let it be repeatedly spread and broadcast in every region of the earth that he has no equal or peer in the spiritual training *(tarbiyya)* of people and their guidance to the Transcendent Holy and Divine Presence!

> *Time swore that it would bring us the like of him,*
> *You have falsified your oath, O Time, so make atonement!*

To Allah be attributed the excellence of the one who praised this Shaykh when he said:

> *A Shaykh who, when he trains, becomes like Ahmad,*
> *And when he speaks, he is like al-Asma'i*

In this same spirit were the following verses composed in his honor by his brother, the meticulous and precise erudite scholar and wonderful poet, the Gnostic knower of Allah *('arif billah)*, Al-Hajj Muhammad *Zaynab* ibn Shaykh Al-Hajj Abdullahi (may Allah be pleased with him):

> *You must know that the Imam has provided and set up,*
>   *a Spiritual Effusion (Fayda) of that which benefits the servants,*
> *At the hands of the medium of Al-Tijani—*
>   *"Barham"—owner of Divine Lights and Gnosis,*
>
> *So everyone of you who loves his Lord,*
>   *will find him pleasing as a Shaykh due to his beneficence,*

Love of his Lord is evidence of loving him,
*   and hatred of Him is also evidence of hating him,*

He inherited the secret of our Shaykh Al-Tijani,
*   from his ancestor—-the best of Bani 'Adnan,*
He revived the Deen after it had become archaic,
*   as well as the Sunna of the Chosen One (Al-Mukhtar) of Banu Mudar,*

He (re)established the Tariqa of our Shaykh Al-Tijani,
*   in our country when the edifice had fallen and collapsed,*
He restored the Tariqa of our Shaykh-the firmly established (al-maknun),
*   after it had been sold for property and money,*

He repaired and rebuilt its structure which had been demolished,
*   and had remained barren and empty for a long time like the Cosmos,*
Allah raised him up for the benefit of creation,
*   and he has deported and banished every destructive and pernicious (rebel) with Truth.*

To where he says:

Attach yourself to him if your want and desire is for Him,
*   and leave every other work and business altogether,*
The chains of transmission (salāsil) of the Shaykhs
*   have been abrogated by him along with the snares and the booby-traps,*

He has educated and trained the disciples in a perfectly beautiful manner,
*   just as our Shaykh Al-Tijani—the giver of bounty and favor,*
Verily, by him the eyes of the sleepers have been awakened,
*   and by him the hearts of the heedless have been enlightened,*

> *On the Remembrance (Qur'an) and the Sunna has the Imam based*
> > *his actions in every desirable way,*
> *So you must submit to him—O Shaykhs of the time,*
> > *unless you have returned to the most odious and hateful abomination,*
>
> *Because in secrets (asrar) he is an Ibrahim,*
> > *and in the Tariqa he occupies a grand position,*
> *So we bear witness to his superiority and preeminence,*
> > *and we are his children in respect of The Truth.*

To where he says:

> *In his presence, O disciple (murid), you will be cultivated,*
> > *and he will provide you with that which is beneficial and useful,*
> *He has frequently trained and educated Shaykhs who had previously deviated*
> > *from the path of right guidance, but then were led aright,*
>
> *Verily, he has come with the authentic spiritual training (tarbiyya Sahiha),*
> > *that he derived from the Sunna—which was explicitly established,*
> *His determination, resolution, zeal and energy (himma) raises the state and condition*
> > *of whoever desires his God—so keep his company if you seek to reach the goal!*

THE DESCRIPTION OF HIS GOOD MORALS AND CHARACTER

As for his modesty and the beauty of his relationship with creation with regard to forgiving and pardoning *(safha wa'l 'afwa)*, generosity *(sakha')*, patience *(sabr)*, equality *('adl)*, dignity *(waqār)*, love *(muhabba)*, trustworthiness *(amana)*, worship *('Ibada)*, loyalty *(wafā')*, compassion *(shafaqa)*, good character with all of the creation of Allah (The Exalted), as well as his strict adherence to the Sunna of the Best of Creation and the Secret of Wisdom *(istinan bi sunna khair al-bariya wa sirr al-hikma)*, he has no comparison, equal or match! In fact, he is the Pole of the niche of these noble attributes and the Key to their doors *(qutb mihrabuha wa miftah abwabuha)*!

As for the pleasing nature of his looks and the purity of his outward appearance, they need no description, for just as his physical self possessed the Divine Beauty *(al-jamal al-ilahi)*—his inner being likewise realized the perfection of the Essence *(al-kamal ad-dhati)*. May Allah not deprive us of the pleasure and delight of beholding him and sitting with him, both literally and metaphorically! From his light, beauty and the cheerfulness of his face, the full moon derived brilliance in the pitch-black night! In regards to his good relationship with creation and giving everyone and everything its right and due and taking upon himself the character of his Lord—The Creator *(Al-Bari)*, The Generous *(Al-Karim)*, The Bestower *(Al-Mu'ti)*, The Guide *(Al-Hadi)*, The Compassionate *(Ar-Ra'uf)*, The Merciful *(Ar-Rahim)*—he possessed a quality that overwhelms the minds of the intelligent! He (may Allah be pleased with him) was observant of the requirements of the afterlife *(shurut al-akhira)* in dealing with close relatives, as well as strangers and he was a guardian of the rights of friends. He realized the utmost degree in humility *(tadaru'i)*, mildness *(khudu')*, asceticism *(zuhd)*, and true devotion *(taqwa)* to Allah, privately and publicly, and in being detached from everything apart from Him, and having a good opinion of Allah and completely entrusting his affairs to Him—until that was witnessed from him by the common people as well as the elite, the near and the far.

Concerning the love for the Messenger of Allah (may Allah bless him and grant him peace) and his Family *(ahl baytihi),* Allah (Blessed and Exalted) favored him with a station which had never been attained nor even hoped for *(lam yadraku wa lā yuram)*! This has been mentioned by the wonder of the age *(a'juwba't zaman)* time, the well-known erudite scholar, the *Qadi* Muhammad ibn Abdullah ibn Mustafa Al-'Alawi:

> *May Allah reward Ibrahim with blessing and goodness for giving benefit*
> > *to the lowliest and the highest in relation to him (al-asl wa'l 'ula),*
>
> *You see them (ahl bayt) spending time in his house (yuqimuna zaman bi darihi)*
> > *and establishing a dwelling there during the stay,*
>
> *There they have no fear of thirst or hunger,*
> > *Nor any fear of being made weary or bored by him,*
>
> *Nor do they fear any humiliation, embarrassment or disdain,*
> > *nor are they afraid of failure and disappointment or anything else!*

To where he says:

> *Among the signs of viceregency (ayat al-khilafa) he bears a sign*
> > *from Allah which is not hidden from those who pay attention,*
>
> *Upon his face is a luminous and radiant light from Allah,*
> > *may Allah refuse to let it be anything but perfect and complete,*
>
> *The two "Abdullah's" played their role in his yield and produce,*

> *for Allah made both of them to be a watering place
> and caused them to drink,*
> *For in the Spiritual Effusion of Divine Gnosis (Fayda 't 'irfan) and*
> *beneficial knowledge, the last resembles the first!*

HIS GENEROSITY AND LIBERALITY

As for his generosity and liberality (may Allah be pleased with him), his beneficence and kindness, the overabundance of his many gifts, his Lordly graciousness *(mawāhibuhu ar-rabbaniya)*, his munificence and open-handedness, they are like the ocean and heavy pouring rain, so he leaves Hatim forgotten and void! May the shawls of gratitude for him never cease being stretched out and his achievements never cease being remembered and narrated!

HIS MOVE TO A NEW VILLAGE AND HIS BUILDING THE ZAWIYA OF AHL DHIKR

At the beginning of his affair he lived in his fathers house in Kaolack. When Allah supported him with help from Himself and caused mankind to come to him from various countries and The Exalted gave him what was not given to any of his people before him and the place became constricted for him due to the multitude of followers holding to his coat tails (may Allah bless them), he established a new village on the outside of Kaolack named *"Medina al-Jadid"*, the home of the unique and incomparable Cardinal Pole *(al-Qutb al-farid)*! He built a Zawiya in it and it was founded on the blessed day of Monday, with fourteen days remaining in the Sacred month of *Dhu'l Qa'da* in the year *1349h* (1929). He completed it in an unusually short time for the construction of such a building, but its owner was for Allah and Allah was for him *(kana lillah wa kana Allah lahu)*-no more need be said! It was made inhabitable by the performance of the five daily *Salat*, the reading of the daily *Wazifa* and the remembrance *(dhikr)* of Allah in the hours of the night, at the ends of the day and at all times (in between), silently and aloud. It became known among the people as *"Zawiya Ahl Dhikr"*-the Zawiya of the people of remembrance! This Medina and the Zawiya has been praised in a poem by *Qadi* Muhammad ibn Abdullah ibn Mustafa Al-'Alawi:

> *The Masjid of Ibrahim is founded upon Taqwa,*
> *and the soil of Medina (Baye) is free of vain talk and sinning,*

I have given up the reins, desperately hopeless from adequately describing even one tenth of his perfections, virtues, exploits, achievements and honorable characteristics. Whosoever is acquainted with his pearls, which sparkle and shine, or is aware of the wonderful benefit and utility which assemble in him, his eye will see and recognize the signs of his preeminence and supremacy, and I am of those who bear witness to that!

> *O Son of Nobility, will you not come close and contemplate what*
> *has been narrated to you, for seeing is not like hearing!*

HIS RELATION TO HIS FATHER

As for his father (may Allah be pleased with him), he was the proof of Islam; the lamplight of the darkness; the protector of the *Shari'a*; the reviver of this Tariqa Tijaniyya after the disappearance of its lights; the restorer of its structure and its minaret after the collapse and destruction of its foundation; the saintly and pious exemplar; the most precise in judgment; the unifier of what had been divided and separated; the master among the preeminent men of this ideal Tariqa; the greatest Shaykh; the renowned and celebrated Sunni-Sufi, our Shaykh and our master, Al-Hajj Abdullahi ibn Sayyid Muhammad. This Shaykh was the compiler and editor of all the sciences, including the branches and the foundations *(al-furu'u wa'l usul)*, especially the Book (Qur'an) and the Hadith. I found a book written by the subject of the biography (may Allah be pleased with him), in which he says that his father had taught the commentary and explanation of the Qur'an or *Tafsir*, to the men of Allah more than a hundred times; performed the pilgrimage, or *Hajj*, and visited the Messenger of Allah (may Allah bless him and give him peace); struggled in the cause of Allah with a beautiful and perfect exertion *(jāhidu fillahi husna mujāhida)*, and that he awakened the eyes of the sleepers.

From the saintly blessing and grace *(baraka)* of this honorable master has come to us all goodness, bounty and felicity. May Allah grant him a reward of goodness on our behalf! His virtuous deeds and exploits, his strength in the *Deen*, asceticism, and piety are too much and too many to be counted or enumerated. May Allah give us and all of our children real benefit from him, and may He pour out His blessings upon us and shower us with His fragrant gifts until the Day of Judgment! *Ameen, Ya Rabbil 'Alameen!*

HIS RELATION TO HIS MOTHER

As for his mother (may Allah be pleased with her), she is the precious and treasured pearl; the priceless gem; righteous; ascetic; virtuous; noble; attentive to the Lordly rights *(huquq ar-rubbubiyya)* in her states and her speech. She is devoted to the behavior and conduct prescribed by the Sunna, to righteous deeds and pleasing actions worthy of thanks and praise. She is the essence of abundant blessing and radiant lights; firmly rooted in capability and certainty; holding tight to the strong and durable rope, our Sayyida A'isha bint Sidi Ibrahim. Ever since Allah placed her under the authority of the father of this Shaykh, she never ceased being concerned for and interested in pleasing him, and striving hard to obey him. She never did anything to anger or injure him, or trouble his mind or the minds of the brethren and neighbors. She never raised her voice above his and she used to behave beautifully towards him, rushing to please him and never opposing him in anything whatsoever. Whenever he gave her advice or instruction, she followed and complied. Her relationship with him never ceased being like this until he was transferred from this life to the abode on high, well-pleased with her and thankful and indebted for her efforts. This has been witnessed on her behalf by the elite and the common folk, by loved ones and by enemies alike.

I have been informed by someone whose words I trust and have confidence in, he being the honorable Sayyid and erudite scholar, the greatest Gnostic *('arif billah al-akbar)*, my master friend and companion, the son of Shaykh Al-Hajj Abdullahi, Abu Bakr—that this mother verbally told him about the following experience: In the 1st month of her pregnancy with this Shaykh, one night in a dream she saw herself standing on something and there was a well beneath her. The moon split from the direction of the East and fell upon her and she became afraid for herself and extremely alarmed because of that. The following morning she came to the father of this Shaykh and narrated the story to him. He scolded and rebuked her and told her, *"Stop that! Say nothing about it and keep it concealed. Do not speak to anyone about that again!"* She also informed Abu Bakr that when she had given birth to the child, the father called her and said: *"Do you have any hope for this son of yours?"* She replied, *"I hope for goodness for him, and that he will become noble, virtuous and righteous, if Allah wills."* The father said to her, *"Yes, I also have determination and intention for that, and I know that it will be, if Allah extends his life and gives us the joy of his survival!"*

I have also been informed by someone else whose words I trust and have confidence in— that he heard it direct from the mouth of the father of this Shaykh, speaking about this mother—that she would give birth to a son who would completely and perfectly inherit from him. He said, *"If not, that will never again be possible for anyone else, because of the women of bygone and previous times, she was their superior."*

HER VIRTUES, DEEDS AND MORALS

As for her virtues, morals, excellence, righteousness and her demonstrating good character with every creation of Allah, The Exalted—Divine Words have no end and all the sheets of paper are not sufficient to record them, not for all eternity! All of what we have narrated here is only as much as time has permitted, due to the absence of leisure and free-time. It has been given generously, but in fear of being long-winded and thereby wearisome to the minds and intellects. What we have concealed, in relation to what we have reported, is like a raindrop in relation to the ocean! Our purpose has been to preserve the secrets and to make them unavailable to outsiders.

We ask Allah, The Exalted, imploring Him by the Presences of Prophethood and Sainthood—that He enable us and all of our loved ones and our brethren to derive from this Shaykh a benefit that is both special and universal, enduring for all of eternity. May His fragrant blessings and gifts return to us and may He pour the oceans of His bountiful favor and support upon us! *Ameen, Ya Rabbil 'Alameen!*

The completion of this summary (of the biography of Shaykh Ibrahim) coincided with the forenoon on Wednesday, with eleven days remaining in the sacred month of *Dhu'l Hijja*, in the year 1352 AH (1933), in Medina-Kaolack (may Allah cause it to prosper and may He keep it safe) Ameen! This was written by the *Faqir* in need of Allah, The Exalted; the one hopeful for his Master to grant him the perfection of Attributes and promotion to the degrees of the Noble, Ali Cisse ibn as-Sayyid al-Hasan ibn 'Andal ibn as-Sayyid Ibrahim (may Allah be pleased with them all).

www.ingramcontent.com/pod-product-compliance
Lightning Source LLC
Chambersburg PA
CBHW021137300426
44113CB00006B/459

9780991381340